# MATERIALS

Written by
Mignonne
Gunasekara

My First
EXPERIMENTS

# BookLife
## PUBLISHING

©2020
**BookLife Publishing Ltd.**
**King's Lynn**
**Norfolk, PE30 4LS**

**ISBN:** 978-1-78637-962-7

**Written by:**
Mignonne Gunasekara

**Edited by:**
John Wood

**Designed by:**
Amy Li

A catalogue record for this book is available from the British Library.

All facts, statistics, web addresses and URLs in this book were verified as valid and accurate at time of writing. No responsibility for any changes to external websites or references can be accepted by either the author or publisher.

To use the QR code in this book, a grown-up will need to set one of these apps as the default browser on the device you are using:

- Chrome
- Safari
- Firefox
- Ecosia

## PHOTO CREDITS

Images are courtesy of Shutterstock.com. With thanks to Getty Images, Thinkstock Photo and iStockphoto.

Cover – sirikorn thamniyom, Kingcraft. Recurring Images (cover and internals) – Buntoon (background pattern), The_Pixel (grid), balabolk (headers and vectors), wildfloweret (boxes), Steve Paint (arrows), yana shypova (speech bubbles), Tsaranna (vector frames and boxes). p1 – sirikorn thamniyom, p4–5 – yadom, Andrey Eremin, Butterfly Hunter, p6–7 – In Green, JIANG HONGYAN, kai keisuke, Lapina Maria, Sakdinon Kadchiangsaen, Tarasyuk Igor, Valentin Valkov, p8–9 – Boris Medvedev, Littlekidmoment, KK Tan, Anton Starikov, Jag_cz, p10–11 – Ligux_f, p12–13 – Marta navarroP, p14–15 – M.Scherbyna, Yuganov Konstantin, Zurijeta, p16–17 – raevas, Salienko Evengii, Nazarova Mariia, p18–19 – GUNDAM_Ai, StockSmartStart, p20–21 – Steve Cukrov, p22–23 – Dean Drobot, Andrey Eremin, Butterfly Hunter.

# CONTENTS

Words that look like <u>this</u> can be found in the glossary on page 24.

# Hello, SCIENTISTS!

Science is about learning why and how everything works. A scientist's job is to find the answers to those questions.

MATERIALS

We are going to be learning about materials today. Science will help us with that, and we'll carry out some fun <u>experiments</u> along the way.

If you complete the experiments, you will earn your Materials Badge!

# Marvellous
# MATERIALS

Here are some materials you may have heard of.

All the <u>objects</u> around you are made of materials. Each material is different, which is why they are chosen to do certain jobs.

Plastic

Rock

Metal

Glass

Wood

Fabric

Some materials are hard and some are soft. Some materials are rough and some are smooth. Materials can be <u>human-made</u>, such as plastic, or <u>natural</u>, such as rock.

**Smooth and shiny**

**Soft and snuggly**

Glass is hard and usually smooth.

Fabric is soft.

Metals can be hard or soft.

Pure gold is a very soft metal. You can even bend it with your bare hands!

# Experiment:
# I LAVA LAMP

Oil and water are two materials that don't mix together.

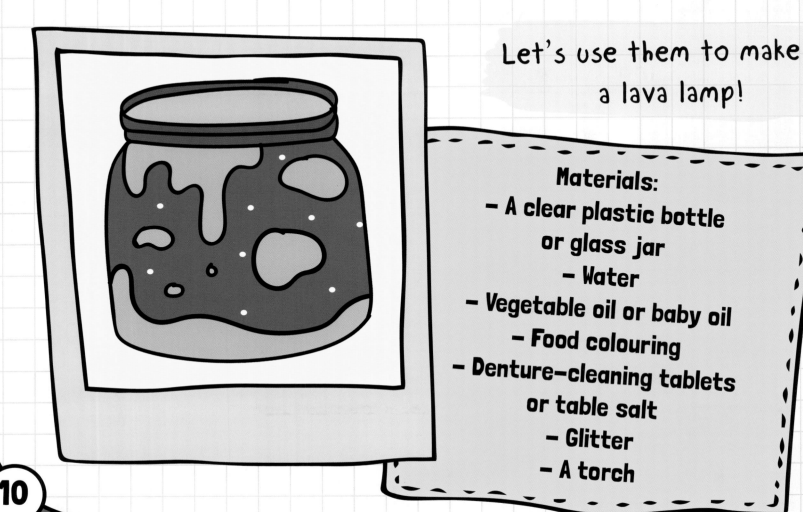

Let's use them to make a lava lamp!

**Materials:**
- A clear plastic bottle or glass jar
- Water
- Vegetable oil or baby oil
- Food colouring
- Denture-cleaning tablets or table salt
- Glitter
- A torch

1) Fill up the bottle or jar with water until it is one-quarter full.

2) Fill the rest of the bottle or jar with the oil. Leave a gap of a few centimetres at the top and let the layers settle.

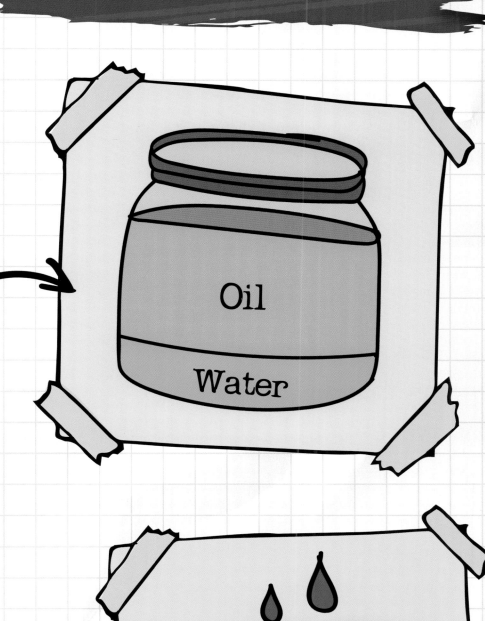

Oil

Water

3) Add a couple of drops of food colouring.

4) Add glitter at this stage, if you'd like.

5) Break two denture-cleaning tablets into small pieces and drop them in. If you don't have any of these tablets, you can pour some table salt in.

6) Your lava lamp is ready!

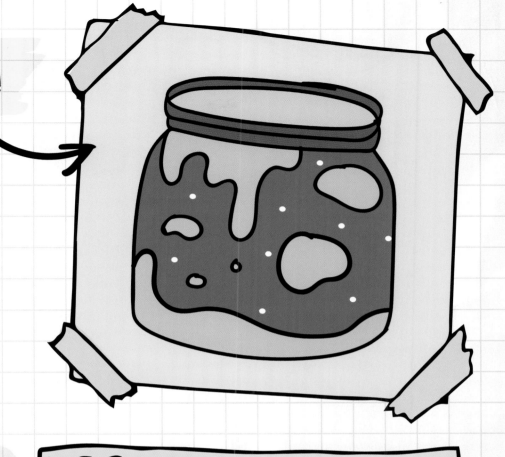

7) You can shine a torch through the bottom of the bottle or jar to make it light up.

When you're done, you can put a lid on your bottle or jar to store it until you want to use it again. Just add more tablets or salt when you want more lava!

**Extra questions:**

What happens if you put the lid on your container the minute you put your tablet or salt in?

What happens if you drop a whole tablet in, instead of broken pieces of tablet?

# Get to WORK

Materials such as plastic, metal and wood are usually strong. This makes them good for building with.

Steel is a type of metal. Steel is used to build bridges.

Glass is used to make windows because you can see through it.

Raincoats, umbrellas and wellington boots are made from <u>waterproof</u> materials, so you don't get wet.

# Making MATERIALS

Natural materials are found in nature. Metals and rocks are found in the ground, and we can get them out by <u>mining</u>. Wood comes from trees.

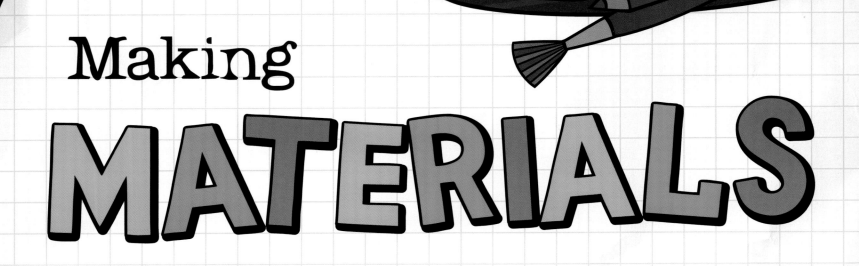

Mining for limestone, a type of rock

Human-made materials, such as plastic, are not found in nature. They are often made in <u>factories</u>.

Plastic pellets

My grandma knitted this scarf out of sheep's wool!

Sometimes, a material is natural but needs a little human help to become useful — such as sheep's wool.

# Ready, Set, RECYCLE

Recycling is really important. We can use materials again instead of making more.

Ask an adult to help you find out which materials can be recycled at your local recycling centre.

PAPER

PLASTIC

GLASS

Glass, paper, some plastics and some metals can currently be recycled.

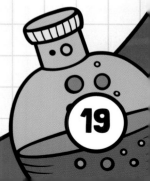

# Experiment:
# CRACKING
## Good Fun

This is a group experiment. You will need eggs, sticky tape and lots of different materials. This could get messy, so ask an adult first.

1 – Everyone take a <u>raw</u> egg.

2 – Wrap your egg in a material to protect it.

3 – Use sticky tape to hold the wrapping in place.

You could try these materials: cardboard, paper, bubble wrap, fabric, sponge, empty toilet rolls.

4 – Everybody drop their protected eggs from the same height.

5 – Make a note of the materials you used and what happened to the eggs in a table like this:

| Name | Egg Cracked? | Material | Height of Drop |
|------|--------------|----------|----------------|
| Liam | No | Bubble wrap | 1 metre |
|  |  |  |  |
|  |  |  |  |
|  |  |  |  |
|  |  |  |  |
|  |  |  |  |
|  |  |  |  |
|  |  |  |  |

**How many eggs cracked? Which materials protected the eggs best?**

# The Badge CEREMONY

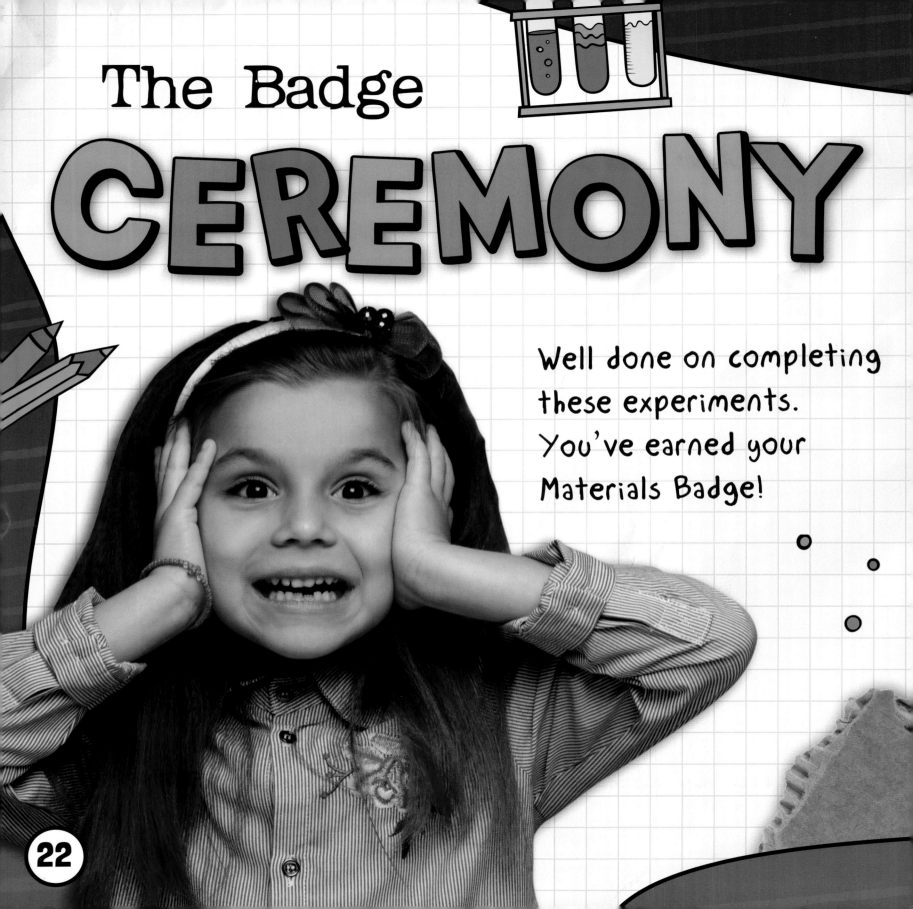

Well done on completing these experiments. You've earned your Materials Badge!

Scan this QR code to download your badge!

# GLOSSARY

| | |
|---|---|
| **experiments** | tests done to explore and try new things |
| **factories** | buildings where things are made, usually by machines |
| **human-made** | created by humans and not natural |
| **mining** | digging in the ground for useful things such as metal |
| **natural** | found in nature and not made by people |
| **objects** | things that you can see and touch |
| **raw** | uncooked |
| **recycling** | using again to make something new |
| **waterproof** | does not let water through |

# INDEX